ABOUT'

Stephen Truelove was born in 1962 at home in Cymmer Porth, in the Rhondda Valleys, South Wales, the middle son of three children born to wonderful parents Glyn and Doreen Truelove. He is father to five, four daughters and one son, and grandfather to three granddaughters and another granddaughter due January 2014.

Stephen is a qualified electrician and aircraft engineer who began his interest in hypnosis in 1999 and qualified as an advanced hypnotherapist in 2002. He continues his interest in training and personal development and is qualified in EFT (emotional freedom technique), NLP (neuro linguistic programming), CBT (cognitive behaviour therapy), Reiki, matrix re-imprinting, time lining, eye movement therapy, the hypno-gastric band and hypnotension; Stephen has also picked up many other tools through experience on his journey. The most recent training Stephen has done is an introduction to Mindfulness.

This work and these tools help people improve and empower their lives, in health and wellbeing, prosperity and being the best that they can be; this is Stephen's passion.

Stephen is also a keen saxophone player who loves bringing enjoyment to people through his music.

Your Unanswered Questions

A journey of discovery and self-empowerment

Stephen Truelove

First published in Wales in 2013

Copyright © Stephen Truelove 2013

The moral right of the author has been asserted.

All rights reserved.
No part of this publication may be reproduced, stored in a retrieval system, or transmitted, in any form or by any means, without the prior permission in writing of the author, nor be otherwise circulated in any form of binding or cover other than that in which it is published and without a similar condition including this condition being imposed on the subsequent purchaser.

ISBN 978-1-492-89811-5

Cover image from Fotolia.com
Author photograph by Catrina Ellen Truelove
Cover design by TheFlowWriter.com

www.mind-set-solutions.co.uk

ACKNOWLEDGEMENTS

My deepest thanks go to my family for all their love, support and patience: to my wife Catrina for your help and letting me practice many of these tools with you; to my five children Nichola, Johanna, Nathalie, Dylan and Kayleigh, who have all had a hand in my successes in different ways – you have inspired me by being the unique, fantastic individuals that you are.

To my grandchildren who bring so much fun into our lives with your innocence and remind me of where it all begins for us.

To my Mam and Dad, who have supported me my whole life even when times have been really tough for you; for me being who I am today, for giving me life, I thank you dearly.

To my sister, Karen, for your guidance through my childhood troubles; and to my brother, Mark, in your passing I realised what an exceptional person you were, I learned so much from you through our experiences growing up.

To my friends and work colleagues for listening to me over the years about my passion for this work, especially Alun, for allowing me to use this material with you and for your continued feedback.

To Helena who helped me during a particularly tough time in my life, and taught me about the Chakra system, helping me control my sensory perception, enabling me to get results quickly, with so many people who come for my help.

To Dr Stephen Gilligan (a student of the late, great Milton Erickson) for hypnotising me and taking me into my well of life to let go of all the unwanted patterns I was unknowingly hanging on to – you changed my life for the better.

And to Julie, who coached me beyond that and helped me release what had been loosened up.

To Jennifer Manson (The Flow Writer) who has come into my life and inspired and guided me through this process to produce this book that will create a ripple effect and help so many more people improve their lives.

To Emma, who has helped me so much to transform my health through her knowledge of nutrition.

To Danusia, for our Reiki exchanges over the past few years.

To all my clients, for putting your faith in me to help you better your lives, health and wellbeing.

To all the people who have touched my life in any way and helped me grow on my journey through this wonderful process of life.

I THANK YOU ALL.

This book is a first introduction to complementary therapy and personal development. It is not intended to be a comprehensive guide nor a substitute for professional advice.

If you have a medical or psychological issue, I recommend that you see your GP as well as exploring the tools mentioned in this book; these two elements complement each other well.

All stories in this book are used with permission.

Table of Contents

Introduction 1
Section two The tools and when to use them 15
    EFT - emotional freedom technique 17
    NLP - neuro linguistic programming 19
    Hypnosis/hypnotherapy 20
    Eye movement therapy 22
    Time lining technique 23
    Matrix re-imprinting 24
    CBT - cognitive behaviour therapy 26
    Subliminal therapy 27
    Reiki 29
    Relaxation through trance 30
    Visualisation 31
    Anchoring a positive state 32
    Releasing uncomfortable or negative feelings 34
    Stepping back from stressful situations 36
    Personal development 37
    Personal productivity 39
    Personal skills 41
    Thinking skills 42
    Being aware of life as a mirror 44
    Sensory energy healing – my therapy 46
Section three The issues and how to help 51
    Bereavement and loss 52
    Addictions 57
    Excess weight 61

Constipation..65

Stress..67

Depression..73

Fears and Phobias...76

Phobias 79

Sexual problems 81

Dis-Ease..83

Fibromyalgia..84

Irritable Bowel Syndrome (IBS)...86

Worry – Real life story...89

Anxiety – Real life story 91

Common issues for university students................................94

Dealing with accusations – Real life story 104

Bad Habits 105

Pregnancy and childbirth.. 107

Self-esteem issues... 112

Jealousy 114

Loneliness... 118

Sports performance - better golf, rugby, football, darts, snooker, tennis, boxing etc. 119

This book is designed to help you by giving you the tools to move you toward a more healthy and empowered life; it contains the building blocks and the first steps to setting you free from limiting beliefs, from limiting behaviours, thoughts and actions which can lead to dis-ease and be detrimental to your health and wellbeing.

After all, where would any of us be without our health?

We are all born with a pure heart; this book is the beginning of taking you back to that place, opening you up to the endless possibilities life has to offer.

It is my belief that we are all here for a reason; my wish for you is that you discover that reason and have all you deserve in health, prosperity, relationships and just being happy with who you are from within yourself.

YOUR UNANSWERED

?

QUESTIONS

Introduction

You have the answers to whatever works or doesn't work in your life!

This book is a guide to help you find the resources you already have within yourself to create and change whatever you want in life, whether it be better health, happiness or wealth.

In it you will find tools that will help you on your journey through life and the multitude of experiences and challenges that are created on your journey.

One of the main ways to tap into the resources you already have within you is to ask yourself powerful questions. These can release the answers you have but don't know you have.

In the different sections you will find stories about people I have worked with, and you will also find lots and lots of questions. When you read these questions, have an open mind. Just let your thoughts float, and see what comes to you.

Being Me (Yourself)

What is this pain inside that I feel?
Is it imagined or it is real?
What goes on within my mind,
The solutions of which seem hard to find?
I really know my issues have roots,
And off these I have grown all these shoots.
If I were to pull these out at their core,
My life I could enjoy so much more.
So where is best for me to start?
How do I tear these issues apart?
If I go back to the beginning,
I am already on the road to winning,
A better life for me,
To laugh and sing and be so free,
To smile more and have more balance,
Because inside I have the resources and talents,
To be more courageous and much more bold,
Because within my soul is the real gold,
So I may be free,
To really be me.

To practice, ask yourself this, and just let your thoughts float as you think about it:

What's the one question you haven't asked yourself yet? The question that will have you set yourself free ...

Many people don't know that they have unanswered questions floating around within them. Others are just plain afraid to even address their unanswered questions because of what might show up.

Looking at yourself is one of the bravest things you can do. Bringing what is deep down inside you into conscious awareness can set you free from limiting beliefs, unwanted behaviours, or dis-ease within your mind and body.

Take your time

You may read this book and choose to resolve an issue today…

Or you may … wait until tomorrow, or the day after …

or next week …

or you may just … leave it to your unconscious mind … and resolve your question in your own time …

Now, do you know that you do know what you don't know that you do know for how to do that?

You have everything you need.

The tools that can help

As well as asking yourself questions to begin to open your mind and think about things differently, there are various tools that have helped me and many others become more successful – whether it be health, happiness or wealth – and they can help you also.

These tools can help you with whatever is happening in your life – anything from bereavement to weight issues, stress, depression, addictions, fears and phobias, worry, anxiety, sexual problems, bad habits, jealousy, loneliness, self esteem issues, to bodily diseases such as fibromyalgia, irritable bowel syndrome, constipation. They have even been used with people with cancer.

These tools can help you with really anything that is or isn't working for you in life.

Some of these tools can be used by you on your own; some of them require a qualified practitioner to take you through the process. I will explain all of them in section two, so you can decide for yourself which one is right for you in any situation.

The answers lie within you, and these tools can help bring those answers to the surface.

Feel your way through yourself

I AM A KNOWLEDGE TREE, I DON'T KNOW EVERYTHING, BUT WHAT I DO KNOW I WILL SHARE WITH YOU.

Please read on.

The three most powerful ways I have come across, through my experiences, to healing yourself, are:

Staying present

This helps you stay aware to your present situations, gives you more energy because your mind isn't cluttered with unnecessary thoughts and chatter.

One way to practise this is when you are driving the car: instead of drifting off to what you are doing that day, pull your thoughts back to what you are doing, what's going on in the road in front of you, other drivers.

Or if you are going into a meeting, instead of planning out what you are going to say, focus on the people around you, and what is happening at the time.

Forgiveness

This sets you free from unwanted emotions you are holding onto – though it has to be true forgiveness from the heart. It's important to feel that you really can forgive, not just say it, but feel it.

If you find this difficult, refer to the section on emotional freedom technique to release the emotions.

Pandora's Box

To all that has ever contributed to my woes,
I know I can choose to just let them go.
Everything was not what it seemed,
It was just the way I made it mean.
So if I could turn another page,
I can let go of all this rage,
Like starting again on a brand new chapter,
A better life I could then capture.
So what will it take for me to transform,
For a better life without any scorn,
To let go of all that has soured,
Leaving me totally empowered.
"Is this possible?" I ask,
And is it really such a task,
To open up those little locks,
And set free the burdens of Pandora's box?

Acceptance

This is about accepting things, people and circumstances, the way they are and the way they are not. It can take some practice at first, if you're not used to it, but once mastered is a very powerful way to approach life.

What's the one question you haven't asked yourself yet, that will have you let go of: this weight, behaviour, habit, grief, anxiety, depression, anger, hurt, guilt, problem, issue, this way of being that is not serving you in your life?

Think of some times when you felt good about yourself. Make a list. Do it now – you can either find a piece of paper and a pen, or sit back with your eyes closed and make the list in your mind.

Many people find this difficult because they seem to focus more on times when they didn't feel good about themselves – but it just takes practice to focus on the positive side.

Understanding your unconscious mind - your first step

Don't think of a blue cat.

So now you are thinking of a blue cat, or at least you are thinking of some kind of cat.

That's how clever your unconscious mind is: when you give it an instruction, like reading the sentence above, it can bring an idea to mind. The trick is, your unconscious mind doesn't understand the word "don't" – all it heard was the idea of the blue cat. So we need to give our unconscious mind positive instructions – not what we don't want, but what we do want for ourselves.

YOUR UNANSWERED QUESTIONS

Now just imagine what influence you can have on yourself when you become more conscious of your unconscious thoughts and you tell your unconscious how you want to think and do things! Instead of your unconscious mind being in control – which is usually outside of conscious awareness – you can tell it what to do, what to think.

You can take back control of your life. Would you like to:

- Get rid of that weight?
- Stop that habit?
- Be free of illness?
- Be successful?
- If you are successful, then become even more successful?

Patterns

A young nine year old was playing a game known locally as "kick-a-tin". In this game, a tin is placed somewhere strategic and one person defends the tin from the rest, who go off and hide. The person defending the tin looks for those hiding and they race back. If the defender is the first one back, the person is caught and stays by the tin, but if any of the others gets to the tin and kicks it then anyone previously caught goes free and it all starts over again.

When the nine year old was the defender of the tin – the rest being older, bigger and some faster – it became quite frustrating as everyone kept being set free and he had to keep starting over and over.

After some time of being the defender, with some of the older boys laughing at him, it all became too much. He began to feel everyone was against him, he felt hard done by, he felt upset and frustrated.

This frustrated feeling was welling up inside his chest. He felt like he wanted to cry, so in order not to show the bigger boys – who were now making fun and laughing more – that he was upset, he ran home.

He was looking for some reassurance from his mam.

"What's happened?" she asked and she listened as he sobbed out the sequence of events that had got him so worked up.

She said "Pull yourself together and go back out and stand up for yourself!"

It was good advice, but not what he was looking for, so in that moment he told himself he was all alone and unloved, and this was a story he told himself again and again through his life.

Just like a seed growing into a tree, that seed of a story became a big tree. It grew many branches on his life journey as he told it to himself in many different situations. It created many patterns and behaviours which in turn brought more problems and issues into his life.

It wasn't until he was in his forties that with some help and some of the techniques in this book he was able to knock down that tree with all its attachments; it was not until then that with the realisation of all the patterns created from that seed that he was able to clear the space for new behaviours and change those patterns that had taken root at nine years of age.

That nine year old boy was me.

What are you holding onto?

What patterns are you holding onto? What stories do you have from events in your life that have created patterns of behaviour that might be holding you back?

I was once asked, "Who are you being?" and things began to change.

My first answer was, "Well, I am being me aren't I"?

But the question means – what sort of person are you at this moment? Who you are being is your conditioning and your programming, and this can be changed: we can choose to be more confident, or kinder, we can choose to be whatever we want to be in any moment.

It wasn't until I let go of some of my own issues that I realised the patterns that had developed through my experiences were creating my behaviours: jealousy, frustration, bitterness, etc.

Once I realised these behaviours did not define me, they were not who I was deep down, I was able to change them. It is such a relief to be free of these life limiting emotions – Phew!

If there are ways of being that you have, that you do not like, they can be easily changed with just a little effort – even things you may not yet realise about yourself!

Letting Go

As you begin to let go of your past,
A new life to be found that I'm sure will last,
Because as you step into this new space,
A younger you will show upon your face.
And if you gaze into your own eyes,
The gateway to your soul, you will find that there lies,
A whole new world for you I am told,
To have and forever in your hands to hold,
So do yourself a favour, I am asking you please,
Begin to chop down all your trees.

Paul's story (used here with Paul's permission)

Paul is a young man who was left brain injured after an unprovoked assault. He spent two months in a coma and thirteen months in hospital in total before going home to continue his recuperation.

He faced many challenges. He was unable to do much for himself – all the things we do and take for granted, the simple things like walking, talking, feeding himself, washing and dressing, had now become new challenges all over again. Paul had lost his independence.

I was introduced to Paul three years after his assault. He had made a lot of progress but there was still a long way to go.

Together we assessed where he was and what he wanted to achieve. This was the beginning of our friendship.

The ultimate goal is to be independent again, to do the things he did with ease before the assault, and to have a loving wife and children.

Although Paul had received much help and continues to do so, it was apparent he was holding onto many emotions – emotions that were understandable considering the trauma that he had suffered.

There was anger, fear, resentment, bitterness. And although they were understandable, they were all holding back his recovery.

We began working together to set him free from these limiting emotions that were attached to his past, to bring him to the point of forgiveness, so that he could move forward.

Progress began ...

How was Paul able to let go of these?

Paul was, and still is, an inspiration to everyone – a brilliant client, and now a friend, who takes on 100% of everything that is taught to him, asked of him, such is his determination to get his life back.

We worked together initially using EFT (emotional freedom technique), NLP (neuro linguistic programming) and hypnotherapy. We also did some Reiki sessions

What are these tools ?

You will find a short description of each of these tools in section two of this book, together with suggestions of when each of them might be useful for you.

They are usually delivered by a skilled practitioner who will help you through whatever is concerning you at the time.

Paul's progress

To be continued ...

Section two

The tools and when to use them

In this section we will go through some specific tools one by one, so you know what they are.

In section three I list out some of the issues people face that can be alleviated using these tools, and suggest ways the tools can be applied.

The earlier tools require that you consult a suitably qualified practitioner or someone with expertise in this area. The later ones can be developed by you to improve your life. In some cases, such as emotional freedom technique, a practitioner can teach you the method, which you can then do on your own.

When choosing a practitioner, ask for recommendations and look for a good reputation. Preferably find someone who has practiced for a number of years. Ask yourself :

> On initial contact do you feel comfortable and at ease with them?

YOUR UNANSWERED QUESTIONS

Do you feel listened to?

Always make sure you work with someone who is suitably qualified and registered with a recognised governing body, e.g. GHR, GHC, NCHC etc, and make sure they are insured for practice.

Ask what sort of experience they have had with your type of issue, and what success they have had.

To use this section of the book, you can either turn to a specific tool that you are curious about, or read them all.

EFT - emotional freedom technique

A suitably qualified practitioner can teach you this technique.

Have you ever heard of Chinese acupuncture, a process where they use small fine needles that go just into the surface of the skin at certain known pressure points of the face and body that activate the energy system of the body?

With EFT we simply use our fingers to activate these pressure points. We tap on them while tuned into an issue, saying simple statements, and thus can take the emotional charge out of events we have experienced in our lives.

I always say, as we start out in life we have a clear field. When we are born, as far as we are aware, everything is ok. As we begin to grow, we learn from our parents, grandparents, siblings, then teachers etc, creating our belief systems and values in life during our early years.

We then begin to have trees growing in our field, representing negative emotions like anger, fear, hurt, guilt, sadness etc, due to experiences and how we perceive them, what we make them mean in our world.

Off these trees grow our branches, our add-ons in life that are attached to our anger, hurt, guilt, and so our stories and dramas begin to mould us.

Many of these experiences have been misinterpreted in our programming. Our subconscious mind stores much of the information that comes in through our five senses: what we see, what we hear, what we feel, what we taste and what we smell.

The purpose of EFT is to take us back to this clear field, so by using EFT persistently – or sometimes you have a one minute miracle – we can begin to knock down these trees. What I mean by this is when we work with a specific issue – let's say anger or fear – we begin to knock down these trees, pull them out by their roots so that these issues and attachments disappear; and very often as you take one tree out others can get skittled out as well!

This then changes our future experiences and behaviours, changing our programming to create a brighter future.

How cool is that?

Where it can be used

Emotional freedom technique can be used on absolutely anything. Just keep tapping!

NLP - neuro linguistic programming

NLP requires a suitably qualified practitioner; some of the processes can be taught so you can later do them on your own.

NLP is a process of talking through issues in a specific way. It sounds really big and posh but NLP is basically about the way we take information in through our five senses, filter it in through our mind and give it meaning based on past experiences.

We have images, some of which are out of our awareness, and we give meaning to these in the moment when we have certain circumstances and experiences on our journey of life.

Many people are living into their past, acting based on past experience, instead of living a new, more empowering future.

NLP has many different techniques that can easily, quickly and effectively re-programme past experiences, enabling you to create a more inviting and empowered future.

Where it can be used

There are so many wonderful techniques from within NLP that can be adapted to free you from many limiting ways and bring more success into your life, in all areas.

Hypnosis/hypnotherapy

This requires a suitably qualified practitioner, or you can learn self-hypnosis.

This is a dreamy natural state of altered awareness. The person goes into a relaxed state where the unconscious mind becomes open to suggestion. The right suggestion can re-programme an unwanted behaviour, habit, or attitude, e.g. lack of confidence etc.

We all go in and out of trance many times throughout the day, for example while watching TV, looking out the window, or driving a car – have you ever said you were "off with the fairies", or "lost yourself" in a book? If shown how, you can become more aware of being unaware and choose how and when you go into trance states.

There are many techniques that can be used within hypnosis.

Becoming more aware is being more in touch consciously, moment by moment, with yourself, your feelings and your thoughts.

I don't mean focusing on yourself every minute of every day, but with a little practice you can be more aware of staying present, so being present in the moment becomes your unconscious state. This state will then put you more in control of your day-to-day life and the circumstances and experiences you encounter, how you react, think and be with them.

Where it can be used

Hypnosis and hypnotherapy can be used with most issues of life, to improve health, wellbeing, prosperity, success, happiness, as well as eliminating all sorts of unwanted behaviours and patterns.

Eye movement therapy

This requires a suitably qualified practitioner to do or to teach you.

This is a series of eye movement patterns, following a sequence of movements with your eyes while at the same time tuned into a particular unwanted or uncomfortable situation/feeling/event.

The emotions that have become attached into any of these situations begin to disappear or change, almost like an etch-a-sketch that erases, leaving a clear screen to start something new and more empowering in the future.

Where it can be used

Eye movement therapy is a wonderful tool for eliminating problems of worry and concern. These can disappear in the blink of an eye.

Time lining technique

This requires a suitably qualified practitioner to do or to teach you.

This is a technique that enables you to travel along your line of life to learn new and useful things.

It can be back into your past, where you can get learnings that may have been missed at that time when the events happened; or you can change the experience in your imagination, so that you experience things differently from now. Old patterns that have formed from those experiences can now be let go or changed.

Or you can travel forward on your line into your future and plant the seeds to create a more empowering, healthy future.

This is a wonderful technique and can yield fantastic results for many individuals.

Where it can be used

Once you identify an incident that may have been at the start of an issue – whatever that issue might be – time lining can be used to change the past experience of bother and concern into future experiences of empowerment.

Matrix re-imprinting

This requires a suitably qualified practitioner.

Matrix re-imprinting is a gentle process. You can begin with a recent memory of an issue and working with a qualified practitioner you can step into that experience in a disassociated way that enables you to keep the original intense emotion at arm's length.

You can then change the elements of that experience as they happened, by using your inner self. Your own inner self or guide will take you step by step gently to the original causes of whatever your issue is all about.

You change the way you feel so that you experience similar experiences that occur in your life in a more positive way from now on.

A combination of EFT and time lining, this process enables you to re-imprint your experiences, enabling you to experience a brighter future. Again, this process produces some remarkable results.

Where it can be used

Similar to time lining, matrix re-imprinting can be used to alter past experiences, leaving you with more peace and calm. Once you identify an incident that may have been at the start of an issue – whatever that issue might be – matrix re-imprinting can be used to transform your experience, in the past, present and future.

CBT - cognitive behaviour therapy

This requires a suitably qualified practitioner to do or to teach you.

Cognitive behaviour therapy is used for issues such as alcoholism, eating disorders, depression, any issue where thought leads to an unwanted behaviour. A client I have worked with found it quite successful for anxiety. It can also give you a better understanding about yourself and the way you think.

The idea is that with these issues, it is the way you think that causes the feeling that leads to the behaviour. With cognitive behaviour therapy you can draw a line in the sand, step over it and live life differently from now on.

Some people get into obsessive thinking patterns or catastrophising thoughts, thinking the worst all the time; this in turn can be very debilitating. Working together you will be able to unravel the patterns and fears resulting from these patterns leading you into a much healthier productive way of thinking that will produce more positive results.

Subliminal therapy

This technique can be learned from Edwin K Yager's book *Subliminal Therapy*.

Edwin K Yager developed subliminal therapy in 1974. It is a hypnotic technique that doesn't require a trance state for use.

Subliminal therapy allows you to access the unconscious and create change within yourself in areas of your life that have become stuck or are not working in the way you want them to.

It enables you to bring unconscious parts of yourself (call them your blind spots) into conscious awareness. This gives you the opportunity to efficiently re-condition or fine tune those parts that are causing the problems.

A part of you knows the answers and what to do to enable you to have better experiences in your future than you had in your past.

The book *Subliminal Therapy* explains in detail.

This is a reasonably easy process to go through and can produce remarkable results.

Where it can be used

Once again, when you ask yourself questions for any issue and trace back the patterns of behaviour, you can use subliminal therapy to create change.

Reiki

This requires a suitably qualified practitioner. Once trained you can practise Reiki on yourself.

This is a gentle healing energy therapy that works with the subtle energies of the body, helping to balance mind, body and heart connections, thus bringing more coherence to the individual.

Reiki involves the practitioner holding hands over the clothed body of the patient, not touching.

Reiki goes where it is needed. It can send energy to a particular area or remove excess energy that can cause imbalances in the system. Imbalances can lead to dis-ease and create complications in everyday life.

Most people drift into a relaxed state while the Reiki practitioner goes through the sequence of the Reiki procedure.

There is no talk therapy with Reiki – just a brief history of your concerns and then leave the rest to the practitioner and benefit from the results that naturally occur.

Where it can be used

Reiki is generally used for situations of physical discomfort and dis-ease.

Relaxation through trance

A qualified hypnotherapist can guide you through this process.

A guided relaxation is a wonderful experience. You will get to a relaxed state that you may have never experienced before.

Using your different senses you can be guided to a safe haven, your peaceful, private place. You can go anywhere you wish through the power of our own mind: a beach, a park, a meadow, a mountain, a room of your choice or anywhere that works for you, and simply enjoy the peace, calm and relaxation – no stress, no tension, not a care in the world – during that period of time, while relaxing through trance. And all the time just sitting in that chair. What the mind perceives, the mind believes.

Relaxation through trance is a very profound experience, available to you when you want to relax. And that is a nice thing to know, is it not?

Where it can be used

Relaxing reduces stress, and with it the impact of any other issue. Relaxation, and relaxation through trance can be used in conjunction with any of the other tools in this book, and is helpful for any specific issue, and for enhancement of life overall.

Visualisation

Visualisation is a great technique to enhance and improve your life and performance.

While relaxed, you can imagine yourself achieving what you want, looking the way you wish to look, even looking healthy.

Just imagine things the way you want them to be, and feel what it will be like when you have that. Then your unconscious mind will develop a path for you to achieve it.

Where it can be used

Visualisation can be used to enhance any area of life.

Anchoring a positive state

You can learn this process and follow it yourself.

One way of changing your state instantly from negative to positive is by anchoring good experiences that you have had to a point on your body.

Here's how it works, step by step:

1. Access good memories and good times from your life.

2. At the same time, push your finger and thumb together – any finger to thumb on either hand.

3. Then make the experience richer visually in your imagination.

4. Any sound, turn it up, make the feeling stronger.

5. Squeeze that finger and thumb together as the good feelings become more intense for a few moments, then relax.

6. Repeat this process with as many good experiences as you can and you begin to stack the experiences up.

7. Then any time you feel less than great for any reason or you need a boost – such as when giving a speech, or facing any challenging situation – just squeeze that thumb and finger together and see

what is different now. Those good feelings flood back and you feel positive and confident.

Wow, what a tool to have, and it is yours forever!

Reinforce it

Remember, from this point on, any time something happens for you and you feel good about it, then in that moment when you experience good feelings, squeeze that thumb and finger together as it's happening and keep stacking all the good experiences.

Where it can be used

Positive anchors can be used to improve your state any time you are feeling out of sorts, for any reason.

Releasing uncomfortable or negative feelings

The best way to free yourself of unwanted feelings is to spend time and face them. Find yourself a quiet, safe space, and try the following:

> Bring the unwanted feeling into awareness and just sit with it.
>
> Thank your unconscious mind for bringing it to your attention.
>
> Then float as if into the centre of that feeling.
>
> Now ask your unconscious mind to intensify the feeling as much as possible – this will allow it to subside more quickly.
>
> Ask your unconscious mind where and when it all began and what is it you need to learn from this.
>
> Give that feeling an intensity from 0 to 10, 10 being the worst it can be and 0 being the best it can be, write the number down.
>
> Then go through the following:
>
>> If that feeling had a colour, what would it be?
>>
>> If it had a shape what shape is it?
>>
>> What about the texture?
>>
>> What about the temperature?
>>
>> Does it move or is it still?
>>
>> Does it have any sound?

Once you have full awareness of this, change the colour to something more comforting, change the shape, get a sense of what happens to the temperature, if it was moving make it still, if it's still make it move, use your wonderful imagination to visualise these changes, or if visualising is difficult for you, then get a sense of the changes.

Think about that feeling, now see how it's changed. You are now changing the state you are in and you can do this with any state any time.

Now rate the feeling again from 0 to 10, and notice how it is coming down.

This can be used in many different cases, issues, whether it be sleep problems, a problem saying no to others, being more assertive or with meeting people etc. There will be a feeling somewhere, created at some time, at some point, because of a decision, which is usually out of conscious awareness.

Your own awareness is the key.

And now notice, as you go through life, how this feeling has less influence over you than before.

Stepping back from stressful situations

This is a very simple strategy for reducing stress, mentioned later in one of the stories.

If there is a situation in your life that repeatedly causes you stress, see if you can take a step back, take a deep breath and take a couple of seconds to collect yourself before you react.

Then see how this alters how you handle it, and how you feel when this situation arises.

Personal development

There are so many ways you can develop yourself: courses you can go on, books you can read, or even just sitting and thinking, and becoming aware of yourself and your thoughts.

It can be very powerful to work on developing yourself, so you can achieve all you want to in life.

Some books I recommend are:

You Can Heal Your Life, Louise Hay
The Celestine Prophecy, James Redfield
The Power of Now, Eckhart Tolle
The Art of Spiritual Healing, Keith Sherwood
Men are from Mars, Women are from Venus, John Gray
The Magic, Rhonda Byrne
The Key, Joe Vitale
NLP Workbook, Joseph O'Connor
Chicken Soup for the Soul 1, 2, 3, Jack Canfield and Mark Victor Hansen
What to Say When You Talk to Yourself, Shad Helmsetter
Ask and It Is Given, Esther and Jerry Hicks
Change Your Life in Seven Days, Paul McKenna
Healing Codes, Alexandra Lloyd Ph.D. and Ben Johnson M.D.
Subliminal Therapy, Edwin K. Yager, Ph.D.
Words that Change Minds, Shelle Rose Charvet
My Voice Will Go with You: The Teaching Tales of Milton H. Erickson, Sidney Rosen

Secrets of the Millionaire Mind: Mastering the Inner Game of Wealth T. Harv Eker

CD

I also have my own relaxation change CD, for creating change through relaxation, which you can get by emailing me at stephentruelove1@yahoo.co.uk.

Personal productivity

This is about your own model of your own world from your own heart, and the difference that makes the difference is you! You can choose to increase your productivity, to make your life what you want it to be.

Whether it's setting goals, being more creative, improving concentration or procrastination, you can achieve, improve or let go of anything you want or wish to be without. Pay attention to your own conversation – many answers are in what you speak, because it comes from your own model of your world, and you are your past conditioning until you gain awareness. Once you gain awareness, change is possible.

Speak positively and life will head that way. We are all good at giving advice to others, but we don't always use our own advice, even when we know it can make a difference.

So...
>What part of your life do you want to be more productive in?
>
>What is it that stops you being more productive?
>
>What goals do you really want to achieve?
>
>What can you change now or later that will give you what you want or help you achieve what you want?
>
>How will you know when you have achieved it?

Breaking down your goals

Why not break things down into smaller chunks so your goals become more easily attainable?

Sometimes we set too big a goal and we lose enthusiasm or motivation because it doesn't come to fruition quickly enough. By chunking your goals into piece parts you will start to see results more quickly and this will give you momentum and motivation to continue forward.

> What blocks your concentration?
>
> What is it that gets in your way?
>
> What causes you to procrastinate around dealing with issues in your life?

We all have the resources within ourselves, and we are all creative in our own way. We just have to find our niche in life. It is within you to achieve your goals. No matter how big or small they are, they are yours, own them!

Personal skills

Being more patient, being the best you can be, your own inner strength, staying cool under pressure, etc. These are all things that can be worked through with incredible results, using many of the tools from this book.

What skills do you have now that you can build on?

Stop and think for a moment, begin making a list.

Ask yourself: -

> What is it I am good at?
>> Am I a good organiser?
>> Am I good at helping people?
>> Am I good at making things?
>> Am I good at something particular when shown how?
>
> What is it I enjoy doing?
> Can I get more from developing what I enjoy?
> Am I good at social skills? If not why not?
> What is it I can do?
> How can I make my life more interesting?
> How can I be more creative with the skills I already have?

We all have skills we can develop whether you believe it yet or not.

Decide what skills you would like to have, then begin to develop them.

Thinking skills

Thinking is a skill; you can do it consciously or you can do it unconsciously, or at best you can consciously create your unconscious thinking and put yourself firmly back in control of your life and health. You can change your self-talk, create more positive thinking, stop thinking the worst and stop over-thinking.

When I am working with clients and I ask, what it is they want, many begin telling me what they don't want. Or when asked to do something differently they will say "I will try and do that". My experience is, when someone says they will "try" and do something or "try" and change something, they usually don't. It is much more empowering to think and say "I will do it" or "I will change it".

Positive thoughts lead to positive outcomes. Ask yourself:

>Where am I negative in my thinking?

>Where am I vague in my thinking?

Decide to act more positively and more definitely.

Useful questions to think about:

>How will I think differently?
>When I think differently, how will things change?
>What thought patterns have I created?

If I couldn't think, what could I do next?

Without thought, nothing is possible, so become more conscious of your thoughts and create the life you want.

What do you think?

Try thinking positively and see what happens.

Being aware of life as a mirror

One thing that people sometimes don't like to hear is that life is a mirror. When something is annoying you in your environment, or in other people's behaviours, that's a message that it's actually sitting there in your own world. This can be a bit hard to swallow, that the thing you find so annoying is really sitting here inside you; once you accept this, however, it can give you a lot of insights and signposts to your own limiting beliefs and limiting behaviours, and seeing those can help you move forward in life.

I often see this in the workplace, where someone will get annoyed over something and someone, yet it doesn't seem to have the same effect on me or others – so it's something for the person who is getting annoyed.

I would say if something like this is happening regularly, that's life knocking on the door, it's a wake-up call. The universal light is always there, always guiding us, but sometimes we just don't see it because of all the clutter we have. Once you see how you are being guided by the things around you, you have the light-bulb moment, and you can use that awareness to move you forward in your life.

I often get asked by partners of hypnosis clients, "When you put them into a trance can I come in and speak to them first?" Isn't it funny how we can see the other person's issues easier than our own, and we want to fix them.

YOUR UNANSWERED QUESTIONS

Just remember, life is like a mirror, what you are seeing over there is actually over here in your world.

Boy that one has bitten me on the arse many times!

Questions to ask yourself if something in your world is bothering you:

> What is it that is in my life that this behaviour or circumstance is reminding me of?
> What is it that I need to look at in myself?
> What is it that I'm not seeing?
> What is it that I need to realise that's having this effect on me?
> What is it that I need to change that will have this annoyance disappear?

Sensory energy healing – my therapy

For this technique, you can work with me in person or via phone or Skype, or try it yourself from the instructions below.

This is a tool that makes you aware of your own energy shifts within your system. These are an indication that something within yourself is going on – they are often linked to your thoughts, and can give you clues about where your blocks are, and what is important to you.

Many people have little awareness of the feeling or energy shifts that happen throughout our day, in the moment as they happen, therefore they don't make the connection between what they are thinking and the feeling attached to those thoughts.

By picking up on these shifts in energy within a person, I am able to help them make these connections, often resulting in breakthroughs and realisations of patterns in their lives, whether positive or negative.

The shifts can be good energy or harmful energy; harmful energy signals that something in your world is blocked for you, stopping you progressing in some area of your life: it might be health – emotional or physical – relationships, finances, work or expression of who you really are. Awareness of these shifts gives us the opportunity to make changes and gain better results in our lives.

Good energy shifts tell you when something is positive for you, and can give you a direction to follow.

An energy shift is a feeling or sensation that lets you know that something needs to be addressed in your world. Just noticing these shifts can help you with how to move forward.

You may already have a sense of what I am talking about – you may suddenly notice that you are happy, or tense, or worried.

Try it yourself. The first step is to increase your awareness of how you feel, notice the feelings that come over you. Then you can use that awareness to become aware of the meaning behind the feeling, and that can give you insight into where it all started – and once you find where it started, the unconscious mind can start to release whatever has been attached.

When you feel a new or strong emotion, ask yourself:

> What just changed in me?
> Why do I suddenly feel this?
> What just happened?
> What was I thinking when the change happened?

A good example would be a smoker – I ask them how they know they want a cigarette, they usually reply, "I had a thought." When I ask a few more questions, they notice a feeling that has been out of conscious awareness. We then go into the meaning behind the feeling, they see the meaning they have added to it, and they can escape from the habit, the addiction.

We are one energy

It's my belief that we are one energy, all around the world. We feel things in each other. This sensory energy process can be done in person, or over the telephone, while speaking with someone on the other side of the world. This proves to me that we are one energy and are all connected in some way.

Job Done

How will you know when your work is done?
Will you still have pain and troubles or will there be none?
How will you feel differently when you are much lighter?
How will it be when your future is brighter?
How will it be when good health has arrived?
Will you do the things that you were once deprived?
How will it be to have a mind so clear?
Will you appreciate your life that is so dear?
How will it be to be free from any dis-ease?
Will you be happy or just really pleased?
When I feel peaceful, happy and free,
That is the way I want my life to be.
When I can say that my pain is none,
That's when I will know that my job is done.

YOUR UNANSWERED QUESTIONS

Section three

The issues and how to help

In this section we will go through some specific issues one by one. You can either turn to a specific issue, or read them all.

For each, there are some questions you can ask yourself to begin to loosen its hold on you. There are also suggestions of tools from section two that might be useful for each issue.

Not everything is covered here – life is very varied, and people face many, many different issues. There should be enough, however, for you to begin to see how it all works, and transfer what you find to whatever it is that you would like to change in your life.

Bereavement and loss

When a person loses someone close to them, through bereavement or separation, it is understandable for them to be sad. I know this myself through the tragic loss of my own brother ten years ago, as well as the loss of my grandparents earlier in my life.

Usually a myriad of emotions become apparent when we suffer a loss of any kind. The question is, how long do we stay in the sadness? How long do we stay in that place that has been created within ourselves?

For some, they become stuck in their emotions and that in turn begins to control their lives.

The first thing is to become aware of these emotions. At the top of the list are usually sadness, hurt, pain, and very often guilt.

Guilt may be surprising, but I find that many clients I work with around bereavement and loss feel guilty. Maybe they weren't there when their loved one passed away, or didn't do or say something they wanted to before they passed, like tell them they loved them.

In the case of a separation they may ask themselves, "What did I do wrong?" So they begin to blame themselves.

This seems a natural reaction for many people.

What to do

If you are stuck in this place of mixed emotions, asking yourself the following questions is a good place to start.

> Is there a reason why I am holding onto this emotion? e.g. sadness – it's okay to be sad, but there comes a time to let that sad feeling go, it's your choice!
>
> Is there anything I would have liked to have said or done that I didn't?
>
> How much longer am I going to stay in this sadness?
>
> What is it going to take for me to let go completely?
>
> What's stopping me letting go of this pain?
>
> Am I ready to let go of this pain? If not, why not?

Many people reflect on what they didn't do instead of what they did do. Try to remember all the things you did right, and be happy about those. You can choose to stay in this painful place or be in a happier place.

> What makes you happy?

Once you've answered that last question, do more of it!

> What are you going to do from today on?

Tools that may help (see section two for descriptions)

EFT, NLP, hypnosis, releasing uncomfortable or negative feelings.

Real life story

Here are some questions I asked a client who had lost her grandfather and turned to drugs to dull the pain:

> *What's stopping you letting that pain go?*
> *What's specific about that pain?*
> *What makes you happy?*
> *How do you know when you feel happy?*
> *You are in control – do you want to hold onto that painful feeling? You have the choice, to have a painful feeling or a happy feeling. You can choose to stay in that sad place or be in a happy place.*
> *What is it going to take to let go completely? It's ok to be sad but there comes a time to let that sad go, it's your choice.*
> *How long do you stay sad?*
> *How do you know it's time to let go?*
> *What's your reason to hold onto pain?*
> *What pay-off do you get from holding onto the pain?*
> *What are you going to do differently from today on?*
> *Are you ready to let go?*
> *If not why not?*

Real life story

This is from a client, Sarah, who had an unsettling dream of her dad dying (he is still alive) and she had never told him she loves him. These questions opened up her mind and allowed her to see a way to move forward. They may help you, too.

> *What is it you need to do?*
> *When are you going to do it?*
> *How will you know things have changed?*
> *What will be different in your relationship with Dad?*
> *What is it you want from Dad? Do you want him to do something that will have you feel his love?*
> *Do you want to hear him say the right words for you?*
> *What is it you are looking for from your dad that will have you be at peace with your relationship?*
> *What will be the one sign that will let you know you have it?*
> *How will life look, feel and be once you have what you want?*

Real life story

Lewys's dad brought him to see me when Lewys was eleven years old. Lewys had lost his way somewhat after his grandmother had passed away. His schooling was suffering with regard to his grades. He had been bullied and his confidence was faltering. Working together using EFT, NLP, and trance work, Lewys made a shift in his attitude resulting in an increase in his confidence. Lewys is now fourteen years old. In a recent conversation with his dad he confirmed that the work we had done together had helped Lewys grow, become more confident and achieve in many areas of his life, including education and sport. He is now a grade A student.

In fact, most children I have worked with have excelled in some part of their lives, in some way, within the following two years.

Addictions

Addictions come in many forms: alcohol, drugs, smoking, spending money, sex, etc…

Most addictions occur due to something missing in our lives. It might be lack of love, fulfilment, not feeling supported, feeling worthless, not loving oneself; we are looking for the "feel-better" factor.

Most addictions relieve a feeling of some kind within yourself, so awareness of what happens before you reach for whatever it is you have become addicted to is the key. It becomes an automatic action: a feeling, related to the issue, and usually unconscious, followed by a thought: I must have a drink, a smoke etc., followed by the action, doing whatever it is you do to relieve the issue.

And so the cycle continues. Until this pattern is broken the addiction will stay in place.

Breaking the cycle

This can be achieved on your own but in many cases help is required to assist with putting in place new patterns to replace the old.

Tools that may help (see section two for descriptions)

Hypnosis, EFT, NLP – and others, depending on what is underlying the addiction.

I recommend working with a suitably qualified practitioner or someone with the expertise in this area. In the meantime, here are some examples:

Real life story – alcohol addiction

These are the suggestions I gave and questions I asked in a session with a client, Craig, who had alcohol issues related to working away from home, and stress around his wedding choices.

> *Choose what you chose, accept the choices you have made, go with it and let go of the rest.*
> *What stopped you doing what you wanted to do?*
> *What feelings do you recognise when you think like that?*

The next part of the session related to the feelings he had – we used an imagery technique so he could think about his feelings in a new way ...

> *What does the feeling look like, what is the colour, the shape, the temperature?*
> *Does it move or is it still, if it moves how does it move? Change it now.*
> *Is the feeling familiar? When was the first specific time you remember that particular feeling?*
> *If you were to feel different, how would that be?*
> *What is it you need to say, do or have that will allow you to let go of that feeling or your behaviour?*
> *Why do you choose to hold on to it?*

What is it you are afraid of?

When is the first time you remember experiencing that?

For the problem to go away, what would need to happen?

What is it you need to do, say or have?

Real life story – smoking addiction

The following comment came during a discussion group on stopping smoking. One group member, now an ex-smoker, said, "When I did smoke I enjoyed every one, in fact I loved it!"

Then he added, "It made me feel relaxed, made me feel calm."

On further discussion he realised that what he really loved was the relaxation and calm, not the cigarette itself.

This is just one way we get tricked by our own mind.

What is it that your addiction gives you, really?

How could you get that another way?

**What's the one question you haven't asked yourself yet?
The one question that will have you set yourself free?**

Who is Smoking Who?

What do you mean? You must be joking!
You want me to give up smoking?
Who are you to tell me so?
It's me who wants to smoke you know.
Or IS IT?
Now I am thinking in my head,
I hear another voice instead,
Just as I thought I would have a roll,
I now know something else is in control.
I don't like it being that way,
It's me who should really have the say,
Whether I quit and make it last,
And not be governed by my past.

Excess weight

These are questions I asked in a group session where one group member told me, "Ok, I would like you to help me lose weight".

Remember that idea of the blue cat? The focus of this question is the weight, even though the request was to lose it. Remember how your unconscious mind is conditioned. If your self-talk is about losing weight, your unconscious mind will focus on the weight and find ways to get it back for you.

That's why so many people have difficulty with yo-yo diets.

So my answer was, "I can help you get rid of the excess weight you no longer want, by helping you get what you want instead. So what do you want instead? If you want to be slimmer and healthier, what is a better conversation to have in your self-talk?"

Questions to ask yourself if you have weight you would like to let go of:

> What is it I'm holding onto?
>
> What stops me getting rid of this weight?
>
> What is this heaviness all about?
>
> What stops me feeling lighter?
>
> Where did this weight issue begin?

What does my daily diet look like now?

What can I do differently than I'm doing at the moment?

What can I change?

What does it look like, sound like and feel like when I am the size and shape I want to be?

How will I know when I'm ready to let go?

Later the conversation in the group came around to him understanding himself, knowing who he really was.

He then said, "But I don't want to know who I really am. I just want to lose weight."

Another group member made a comment, "If you don't know who you are, how are you going to change anything?"

It's a good question, who was he? What do you think?

If you have weight you'd like to let go of, ask yourself:

What's the one question I haven't asked myself yet, that would have me let go of this weight?

Being Lighter

A stone here, a stone there,
Lots of blubber everywhere.
All those people, all that sound,
As they say, why do they choose to be so round?
Is it an illness if so an excuse,
Or is it bad choices for weight to produce?
How did I do it? What did I say,
That changed something inside me and got me this way?
So wait just a minute!
If I am to blame,
Then one thing is for sure I can do just the same.
If something inside listens to what I say,
Then I can re-programme and be a new way.

Real life story

A client came to get rid of excess weight she was carrying. After three sessions she was a bit disappointed that she was not seeing or feeling a reduction in her weight, shape or size.

The issue/pattern was beginning to emerge of her good feelings when eating cakes, etc. She then connected the memory of when she was a small child, she and her dad would make it fun to sneak some cakes after they had had their meal.

Her dad was now passed and a part of her was getting some pay-off by eating the cake and trying to get those same feelings she used to experience.

With her connection to the pattern and some work to complete with the loss of her dad, she began to let go of the excess weight that she was finding a problem. Her eating habits changed and she became happier.

Tools that may help (see section two for descriptions)

Hypnosis, EFT, NLP – and other techniques according to what is underlying the issue – have a look in section two and see which ones appeal to you.

Constipation

Much like weight, constipation is something you are holding onto, something you are just not letting go of.

When something is a concern or a bother to us it throws our system out of balance. When your system is out of balance, parts within you don't function properly; there is tension of some kind.

When relaxed and brought back into balance, the parts work properly again. This sounds really simple, and most things can be, but we as human beings sure can make things complicated.

I have had many clients who have suffered constipation, although that's not usually what they have come about. After working through and clearing some issues, however, relief in this department is found.

Constipation no more, and what a relief that is!

Questions to ask yourself:
- What am I holding onto?
- What am I scared to let go of?
- What have I let build up in my life?
- What stops me letting it go?
- Is there anything I can do differently to feel a different way?

What is it that's really stuck in my life? What is holding me back?

Tools that may help (see section two for descriptions)

Hypnosis, EFT, NLP, and others depending on what the underlying issue is – and just going for a walk!

Once you have answered the questions above, some other issue may arise, and you may want to look at another part of this book to find help with that.

Stress

Dr Alex Lloyd, in his book *The Healing Codes,* tells us that stress is one of the main causes of illness and dis-ease. Stress is caused by an energy problem in the body and the best thing to combat stress is an immune system working at its best.

With a balanced mind and body and balanced nutrition, you can move mountains.

Stress is a naturally occurring thing. We all need some stress in our lives to function, but what happens when we become over stressed or over stretched?

There are so many stressors in modern day life – external factors like running a home, finances, work, family, other people or situations you just find yourself in or a part of.

Awareness and communication can be key in helping with stress issues.

Awareness

Becoming consciously aware of the triggers you have for stress can help you. Once aware, you can make changes in your environment and surroundings or you can make changes internally in your thinking by changing your self-talk.

How can you tell if you are stressed? You may notice an internal change like an uptight feeling somewhere in your body or in your head; it could be externally in the form of a rash, skin itching, and hot flushes.

Everyone has their own signals that tell them they are stressed.

What do you normally do when you feel stressed? Think about it for a moment. Do you react, or do you have strategies to cope with it?

The first thing is to eliminate the triggers, and then alter the behaviours and patterns that you have in response to stress.

Ask yourself these questions:

How do you know when you are stressed?
Where is the feeling that you are stressed?
What do you say to yourself when you begin to feel stressed?
Do you become angry, agitated or fired up?
Do you withdraw into yourself and get depressed?
Do you seek company or do you like solitude?

Real life story

I had a client who would go into panic mode if someone approached her in a vehicle or as a pedestrian to ask for directions, which would then leave her feeling stressed.

This is an example of an internal reaction to an external event.

Together we worked out a strategy that whenever someone stopped and asked her for directions, she would take a step back, take a deep breath and take a couple of seconds to collect herself.

Since then my client has coped really well in these types of situations. She also realised other parts of her life were being affected in this way (as before, a pattern of behaviour can be like a tree, with many branches). She used the same strategy in other situations and has become more confident in dealing with people in general.

How simple was that? There were no in-depth therapy tools used, just the simple strategy of taking a step back and giving herself a moment to collect herself.

Many clients I work with report they already knew what the problem was, they just hadn't realised how they had put their patterns in place, or how to work out strategies to overcome them.

Very often remedies for over stress can be quite simple.

Self-talk

Your own self-talk is so important. The more consciously aware of your unconscious thoughts you become, the more you can control your response to things that have previously caused you stress.

Allowing others to help

If you communicate to others around you that you feel stressed and what's triggering it, you can work together to eliminate the environmental factors that may contribute to your stress.

This can especially apply to stress in the workplace.

Even just talking the issue out can be very helpful.

Workplace stress

This is just a label, why not stress as a house-wife or stress in the supermarket or stress with children?

Stress is stress wherever you are, it is a state that gets triggered whenever your buttons get pressed. It is due to whatever is going on in your environment wherever you are at any given moment in time.

But it isn't always the same. Sometimes the thing that stressed you out yesterday doesn't stress you today. You can choose the state you are in regardless of what is going on in your surroundings.

If you ask yourself some questions, you can increase your awareness and work out ways to deal with it.

> What happened differently?
> What did I do differently?

What caused me to choose a different state and react to the same situation in a completely different way?

Once you recognise the buttons that trigger your emotions, that cause your stress response to kick in, to the point where stress causes you problems, you can free yourself from over stressing in situations that you used to.

Stress-Less

What is life when full of stress?
It's on the news and in the press.
Now I don't mind a bit of pressure,
But hold on now, it's become a stressor.
So what if I can breathe so deep,
Whenever I feel that tightening creep,
Upon my body and my mind?
Deep breathing helps release I find.
So when I feel that stress through the day,
I will deal with it in my new way.
Take a step back and deep breathe I will,
It's better than taking any pill.
When I know what makes me stress,
Then of that I can do less.

Tools that may help (see section two for descriptions)

You can create a positive state using anchoring. As with most other issues, hypnosis, EFT and NLP are the mainstays of therapy. Relaxation through trance is also excellent.

Or you can just take a step back, like my client did.

Depression

How do you know you are depressed?

Depression came on me at the time of my divorce, with the fear of losing my children. I hated not being there for them in the nights. For me, depression was a dark low feeling deep in my chest and stomach. A feeling of worthlessness.

Nothing seemed to matter, I didn't care about anything or anyone, including myself. I sat for days on end in jogger bottoms, staring into space, lost in my own thoughts and self-pity, feeling very sorry for myself.

Some say when you hit rock bottom there are two ways: out or up.

I now know that when we have the know-how, we can come up from the bottom of any despair or situation we find ourselves in – you do know how.

Mind and body can break you or make you, and when you are in control of your own mind and body and they work together, you can achieve anything – and I mean anything – you choose.

Often anxiety underlies depression, in which case if you deal with and release the underlying anxiety then you will release the depression, too.

Many depressed clients I have worked with have had underlying anxieties from some issue from their past, and once realised and released their depression is lifted.

Often they are surprised at the event or events that have caused and triggered their downward spiral to that darker place – but we condition ourselves to go there so easily.

Once you know how you do it you can start the building blocks to bring yourself out of that pit and stay out!!

When you are consciously aware of your internal thoughts and feelings there is always a therapy tool that you can use to bring yourself up again.

For me the word depression is something being pushed down. Well, no one or no thing will push me down again, I will get up and rise above it.

Here are some questions to ask yourself that may help:

> How do you know it's time to be depressed?
> What states do you pass through to get yourself depressed?
> What pay-off do you get when depressed?
> > Do you get more sympathy?
> > Is it a way of avoiding upcoming situations or events?
> How long do you choose to stay depressed once there?

What changed to bring you out of that depressed state in the past?

> Was it your thoughts?
> Was it something in your environment?
> Was it something you heard someone say or something someone did?
> Was it something you did?

How do you know it's time to change that state?

What does it feel like when that depressed feeling lifts?

What is it you can be responsible for that will keep you in a better state?

What is it that lets you know it is ok to be ok?

Techniques that can help lift depression (see section two to understand more about these)

Hypnosis, EFT, matrix re-imprinting, CBT, and NLP.

EFT once learnt can be used by yourself; the rest will require assistance from a suitably qualified practitioner. All therapies help you move toward the same result, in this case to free you from that awful down feeling we call depression.

When used skilfully, combinations of the above-mentioned techniques can help quickly lift depression; then with your new knowledge about how to enter this healthier state you can keep yourself in your new state – whether it be happiness, calm, peacefulness or just feeling alive inside.

Fears and Phobias

It is said that we are born with only two fears: fear of falling and fear of loud noises. All the rest is learnt – so can be unlearnt.

Whether yours is a fear of spiders, death or public speaking, they are all learned. Here are some questions that may help loosen the fear:

>How and when did you learn yours?
>Where is your feeling of fear? In your head or body?
>What do you do that keeps your fear in place?
>What is your pay-off for keeping hold of your fear?
>>Does it protect you from something?
>>Does it give you an excuse not to do something?
>>Does it give you attention?
>>Do you get sympathy?
>What will life be like without your fear?
>How will you do things differently?
>What will you be able to do, or do differently without that fear?
>How will you know this fear is gone?
>What has changed?
>What will now be possible without that fear feeling?
>How much calmer are you without that fear?

Tools that may help (see section two for descriptions)

Hypnosis, EFT, NLP, matrix re-imprinting, time lining, Reiki and CBT are all great techniques to alleviate fears when used in the right ways.

You could also try the following, a variation on the releasing uncomfortable or negative feelings process from section two – it involves bringing the fear up, so you may be a bit uncomfortable. Find yourself a safe space where you won't be interrupted.

> Ask your unconscious mind to bring your fear feeling forward
> Thank your unconscious mind for bringing it forward.
> Now rate your fear from 0 to 10, 10 being the worst 0 being fine.
> See if you can intensify that feeling – this may seem a bit of a strange thing to do, but it is part of the process.
> When you have that feeling at its most intense, ask yourself, where, how and when did it originate?
> Pay attention to any memories that may arise. Sometimes awareness of the first sensitising event can dissolve the fear.
> Alternatively, ask yourself, if the feeling had a colour, what would that colour be? If it had a shape, what would that be? If it had a temperature, what would that be? Does it have any sound? Does it move or is it still?
> See if you can change these elements, change the colour, the shape, what happens to the temperature? How does it change?

> What happens to the number now when you rate it from 0 to 10?

You have now started to change the neural pathways that have kept this fear in place. Well done, you!

Over the next while, observe how your fear changes or lessens.

Phobias

Phobias are fears that have got out of control and are controlling you. Fascinatingly, many phobias have nothing to do with the presenting problem, for example fear of flying may have started with something else, such as fear of the dark, confined spaces (there's that tree again).

Again, once made conscious of the pattern you have created, the phobia can be lifted. The following questions may help:

> When did these feelings begin?
> What was going on in your life at that time?
> Was it someone else's reaction to something or your own?
> How will life be different without this phobia?
> What stops you letting go of this phobia?
> What will happen if you do?
> How will you know the phobia has gone?
> What will change in your life when you are free of your phobia?
> What benefits will you have?
> What will you be able to do differently?
> Can you live your life without this phobia?
> What possibilities will open up in your life that weren't possible before?

Tools that may help (see section two for descriptions)

NLP, hypnotherapy, EFT, subliminal therapy, time lining, eye movement therapy.

In my view and from experience, the best, quickest and permanent way to resolve your phobia is with the fast phobia technique from NLP – it is also known as the rewind technique; even more powerful is using this technique through hypnosis. Major phobias have been completely resolved in a one hour session. For this you need a qualified practitioner.

Real life story

I recently worked with a client, Jason, with a very strong spider phobia. Even talking about spiders would cause his face and head to go red, his temperature would rise and he would start scratching profusely.

His wife also had a phobia of spiders, and guess what? They have two children who have picked up the learned behaviour, and have the same phobia.

This intense spider phobia was resolved for Jason in a one hour session using EFT and the rewind technique while the client was in trance. All his symptoms have alleviated with no recurrence, and he is now able to do everyday tasks which were big issues for him before this session, without any of the previous discomforts, when spiders would appear in his environment.

Sexual problems

When people have issues in the bedroom: lack of libido, loss of sex drive, can't get it up, whatever, the problem usually lies outside the bedroom.

Somewhere along the line, something has occurred that had an effect on our system, and back to our tree and branches idea of a pattern of behaviour or response, it has spread to affect this area of life, too.

It might be a decision you made, a belief or part of your values system.

Ask yourself

> When did this issue begin?
> What was happening in my world at the time?

I am sure that at one time things in the bedroom department were ok, then something changed, something happened, internally or externally, to change your thinking, your reaction or behaviour towards sex.

> As you think about it, do you get a feeling or a sense?

Use that feeling or sense, take a quiet moment to reflect, allow that sense or feeling to take you to where the problem originated. Follow the feeling and you will get insights as to what is really going on.

Ask yourself questions about your issue, then forget about the question, and wait for your unconscious mind to provide the answer, just like it has done many times before now, in other situations.

The answer may come straight away or within a couple of hours, or even a couple of days, when you least expect it.

If the answer hasn't come in a couple of days, ask the question of yourself in a different way or ask a different question.

What's the one question you haven't asked yourself yet that would have you resolve this issue?

Keep repeating this process until the answer comes – and it will.

Just trust your unconscious mind, because it is there to help you and to look after you.

Sometimes there is resistance to change, because whatever is going on was designed in the first place to protect you. Once you outgrow the need for that particular way of being, the unconscious needs fine tweaking or slight re-programming so you can move on.

Alternatively, rather than follow feelings or senses back, just give it up, let it go, and live in the moment right now. Sometimes just relaxing about an issue will allow it to resolve on its own.

Dis-Ease

I say dis-ease because your mind or body or both may not be at ease about something.

This Dis-Ease

This problem, this hurt, this pain that I am feeling,
From all to be freed does seem so appealing.
So as I consider, what will it take,
For me to let go and be free of this ache?
Because all of these troubles within me reside,
And like a cancer do eat me inside.
So what can I do to put things to bed,
All of these things that go on in my head?
Why do I feel this deep inner unrest?
What will it take for me to be at my best?
How will I know that it's time to let go?
What if this magic can really be so?
What can I do and what can I say,
So that my life can be this new way?
So give me the answer I am asking you please,
To have life a new way, so peaceful and at ease.

Fibromyalgia

Fibromyalgia causes discomfort within the joints and can be very painful and disruptive. So far there is no medical answer or reason for this condition.

My belief is that there is an answer somewhere within you. Most people have the answer and resources within themselves to free themselves from dis-ease, though it may take some time and effort, a willingness, and an open mind to think, look at and feel differently about yourself and your world.

Ask yourself the following questions to start to get to the bottom of it:

> When did this discomfort in my joints begin?
> What was going on in my life at that time?
> Were there any painful events or situations going on?
> Were there any unhappy relationships in my life?
> Is the discomfort worse at any particular time of the day or night?
> What is the difference when there is no discomfort?

If I were doing a session with you, I might ask you the following:

> How do you make the discomfort start?
> What are you thinking and doing or not thinking and not doing?
> How do you make the discomfort stop?
> What happens for it to start again?

What will life be like without that discomfort?

What is missing in your life?

When you are in a happy place there is no discomfort – so what makes you happy?

Once you know what makes you happy, do more of it!

Tools that may help (see section two for descriptions)

EFT, hypnosis, subliminal therapy, CBT, matrix re-imprinting, reiki, time lining.

Relaxation in a happy, safe, peaceful place in your mind can ease the discomfort of fibromyalgia.

Practising EFT on your symptoms can relieve fibromyalgia, but you may have to be persistent. Go to a qualified practitioner to learn the techniques, and keep tapping on any new issues that arise from the old or previous aspects of this condition.

Persistence is the key with EFT – just keep on tapping.

Some people will have a one-minute miracle with this technique with some issues, while others may take a while longer.

Irritable Bowel Syndrome (IBS)

I was once diagnosed with IBS and I accepted what I had been told by a consultant at that time.

Dr Stephen Gilligan, Ph.D., a licensed psychologist, stated at a conference that he no longer diagnoses his patients because it puts them in a box. When diagnosed you become fixed on the idea that you have that problem. The problem can become exacerbated, and you tend to look for remedies specific to that diagnosis.

My IBS was put down to mainly diet, specific foods and drinks, that caused my unbearable feeling of discomfort and occasional vomiting. I accepted that and avoided these items, yet I would still spend many nights slumped over the corner edge of our kitchen worktop as this was the only way I could get relief of my symptoms. This would then cause sleep deprivation and leave me unable to function properly the next day.

After going through many therapy processes and acquiring many of the tools described in this book, I hit on a few different decisions and events from my past that had been at the cause of the issue.

Once I became aware of these, all my symptoms reduced. I had diarrhoea for a day or two but unusually didn't feel the usual weakness or tiredness associated with it. From that point on all my symptoms related to IBS disappeared, dissolved, went away, gone. How brilliant that was!!

When the mind and body are not at ease or balanced this can cause tension or tightness of different organs within the body; the release I had from patterns of my past conditioning put my body back at ease.

That was eight years ago, and I now eat and drink all the things that were said to cause my IBS and I haven't had the symptoms back again.

Ask yourself:

> What's the main cause of my IBS?
> What are my thoughts that I may not be aware of when my IBS kicks off?
> What happened in my life to cause tension in my body?
> What was it I didn't do or say at that moment?
> What is it that makes me tense inside?
> How can I be more relaxed inside?
> What is it I could be more aware of?

What is the one question you haven't asked yourself yet, that will have you be free from your IBS? What stops you letting go?

Tools that may help (see section two for descriptions)

Relaxation through trance will help your mind and body to be more balanced and relaxed. How can you be relaxed and tense at the same time? Try that one out and you may find that you cannot.

Reiki is especially good for balancing mind, body and spirit. All the techniques in this book can alleviate the symptoms of IBS. A combination of these techniques may result in complete resolution of your symptoms.

Hypnosis can be used to help you imagine a coating for the gut that will protect you from the irritation that causes IBS.

Worry – Real life story

In a group I recently worked with, one person asked, "How do I stop worrying, because I worry all the time about most things – well it's natural to worry isn't it?"

Me: Has any of that worry ever helped you to resolve anything?
Client: No, I suppose not.
Me: So what distress has all that worry caused you?
Client: Lots.
Me: Then what's the point of continuing to worry from now on?
Client: I suppose.
Me: Isn't it easier to do something, anything that may change the situation somehow, instead of sitting and worrying about something you may never be able to do something about?
Client: Hmmm.
The client has now gone into a different enquiry inside. Will things now resolve or will the client continue to worry? It's up to them.

It is your choice and always is.

Worry

Worry, worry all the time,
Wouldn't it be better if all was fine?
But that is not the case you see,
Things they always worry me.
What did worry ever get?
Heartache, pain and much more fret.
Someone out there tell me please,
Does worry ever bring me ease?
When I think of worries of the past,
Oh, how those worries they did last.
All the things I've worried about,
Has anything resolved or cleared out?
No! Worry has never solved a thing,
But always action to be taking,
That will put me more at ease.
So start doing instead of worrying,
I ask you please.

The exercise on the next page, about anxiety, may also help with worry. For further ideas, go to the section on resolving uncomfortable feelings in section two.

Anxiety – Real life story

In another group situation we spoke about anxiety:
Group Member: I get anxiety attacks.
Me: How do you know you get anxiety attacks?
GM: Because I panic.
Me: What happens when you panic?
GM: I get afraid.
Me: When you get afraid, how does that make you feel?
GM: I get a feeling in my chest.

Bingo!! We then work with this feeling in the chest and ask questions to trace back the memories of where the initial event started everything off – which is usually totally unrelated to what is going on at the present time.

Once this is out in the open, very often the panic and anxiety will dissolve.

An exercise to try

Become aware of the feeling, wherever you experience it – in the case above it's the chest area. Ask yourself, if it had a colour, what would that be? If it had a temperature, what would that be? If it had a sound, what would it be? You can loosen the anxiety by seeing if you can change the colour, temperature, sound, to something more pleasant, something more comfortable.

Tools that may help (see section two for descriptions)

NLP, EFT, hypnotherapy, reiki, matrix re-imprinting, subliminal therapy.

The exercise above is an NLP technique. You can also use EFT or hypnosis with a qualified practitioner to get to the root cause of the anxiety; then you pull out your tree by its roots and many other attachments disappear, too, putting you firmly back in control of your feelings, reactions and your life.

Most of the time, the answers we find to our issues are trivial and no real surprise; the biggest surprise is realising the patterns and how we have formed and linked experiences that have created the issue in the first place.

Real Life Story

A client came to me a little while ago with an anxiety issue. She reported she had recently split from her husband after him having an affair. What she had realised after working through things initially on her own was that there were things she had to take responsibility for.

She realised how she had pushed her husband away in the relationship: sex and intimacy were nonexistent and she kept him at arms length. So there was no proper communication and they were not relating to each other. Obviously, him having an affair was not the answer either.

We worked through some initial issues with EFT and NLP and then used hypnosis. Many patterns (trees and branches) began to emerge. One most significant event was when she was five and had sustained a broken leg.

She was only able to get about during that time in a wheelchair and had someone who would take her to places such as school. On one particular day this person had walked away for some reason and left her; she sat watching this person going away and at that moment she felt distressed about her whole situation, and made a decision about herself and other people. "People would leave her so it was safer to not let anyone too close." Her tree was formed.

The other person had done nothing wrong – they were just tending to something else – but the decision made about what was going on in the five year old world was the start of many unconscious patterns (branches).

From then on my client would stay in her head because if she went into her heart it made her vulnerable and this would cause pain, hurt and suffering – this is common for many people.

Once she realised this was the root of the issue, she could then see many patterns with other relationships and within work etc.

With a little help, she was able to change in ways that best suited what she really wanted from her life.

Common issues for university students

Depending on your situation, university can be a tough, sometimes scary time. Being away from home, learning to handle money, fitting in, etc. – and that's without all the studying and hard work that has to be put in.

For some, there is fear of failure or fear of the unknown.

For others it's exciting, and they just love it.

Some students lose their way, unsure if they made the right choices: choice of university, choice of course, whether they actually want to do what they started out on once they complete their time at university.

It is a life changing experience.

Wherever you fit in this, remember you did choose to be where you are, and it will all turn out okay.

A clear mind, staying present, and "coming from nothing" all help. Let me explain what I mean by "coming from nothing"...

When we meet people for the first time, our previous experience can influence what we think of them; it helps if instead of that, we can come from a clear place, with no judgements, no expectations or self induced pressures.

Just staying present and focused on what you are there for and being who you really are is key.

Many students become confused over: "What's it all really about? What's my next step? What if I don't achieve what's expected of me? etc." This in turn begins to trigger issues that can for some become overwhelming, and cause all sorts of insecurities, anxieties, and even depressed states.

Have a look through this section of the book for other things that may apply to you, and may be helpful to read about.

Tools that may help (see section two for descriptions)

Hypnosis, time lining, NLP and EFT (to take out the feelings that have been attached) can help, bringing out your natural learning, giving more clarity and assisting you to refocus on your goals and outcomes, to achieve your degree and prepare you for your next step forward in life beyond your degree, whatever that may be for you.

Visualisation can also be very helpful with focusing on and achieving your goals.

Confidence and self-belief

How well you learn is mostly about self-confidence and self-belief. You can do it if you believe you can do it. With your own self-belief in place, anything is possible.

Following any of the self development tools in section two will help you build your confidence.

Learning to learn

I have helped people from six years old to eighty six years old around their learning issues. There is always something to learn and we are always learning.

Learning is natural – it's just a matter of finding out how you learn – because we all learn differently.

If you have issues around learning, there is usually something else causing it. Finding out what is the cause of the disruption to your learning pattern is what helps to move you forward.

Real life story

When I started Infants' School at four years of age, after a couple of days, at the start of the morning, the teacher – who was an elderly lady – gave out a box of crayons to every child, putting them on the desk in front of each child and saying not to open them until she said.

I was the youngest in the class at this time and felt excited, so I opened my crayons. Next moment, she hit me across the back of the head and put me at the front of the class facing the blackboard. I was crying and some of the children were laughing.

It wasn't until I was in my 40s that I was able to take out my tree from this moment, a tree that had grown many branches.

Whenever I would be asked to work something out on the blackboard from then on, my mind would panic and freeze. The more the teacher got annoyed, the more I would feel panic and the more muddled I would feel.

As I grew up, it affected my sport – football – and other parts of my life, being afraid of getting something wrong. Even with darts, which I played for a while, I would panic when I got down to lower numbers and would have to think of how to have a shot out, how to work out what numbers to aim for – with the small blackboard at the side of the dart board, and everyone else behind me.

It was only during a 10 week course that I got complete with this. I had previously, at another course, stood up in front of everyone and presented something okay; on this course I had planned to get up and speak, but the person presenting the course announced he was a teacher. Immediately the room closed in, my panic and my fear welled up inside. I wasn't going to stand up in front of this teacher, and what I now saw as a class.

It took me five weeks to find the courage and stand up in front of everyone and share my story. I then looked across at the presenter (teacher) and said, "I am not afraid of you any more" and I felt the freedom in that moment from all the patterns that had formed from that four year old. It was one of the most enlightening feelings I have had.

After sharing this, four people put their hands up and thanked me. What was it I had done that they wanted to thank me for? Well, in my sharing of my experience, these people, and maybe more, were able to connect with the same or similar experiences, behaviours, patterns, in their own world. One quoted: "I now have the courage to share my experience, now that Steve shared that experience."

Sharing is so powerful.

To help with your learning, ask yourself the following questions – because you already have the answer, inside you:

> How can I learn more easily?
> What can I do to make information stick?
> What do I already know?
> How can I learn differently?
> How much more do I know now than I did six months ago?
> What have my past experiences taught me?
> How can I do things differently so as not to make the same mistakes again?

Something that is useful to know when it comes to learning is what your main representation system is – how you operate, how you learn differently.

There are several main learning systems, and we all have one that we naturally use more. The main learning systems are: visual, auditory and kinesthetic. Most people use more than one system at different times and to different degrees, but one will dominate. Once you know the main system you generally operate from, you can practise using other systems by paying attention to the way you experience the world, and the words you use.

To work out which system is your main one, have a look at the following sets of words. Which ones do you usually use to describe your experience?

Visual words

Illuminate	See	Focus	Imagine
Clear	View	Picture	Reveal
Bright	Look	Take a peek	Tunnel vision
Dim	Appear	Outlook	Watch
Scene	Picture	Sparkle	Mirror
Perfect	Gaze	Vivid	Dim

Auditory words

Hear	Hush	Resonate	Call
Listen	Sound	Say	Rhythm
Deaf	Tune	Noise	Loud
Silence	Pitch	Echo	Quiet
Tell	Volume	Shout	Talk
Roar	Melody	Ring	Accent

Kinesthetic words

Touch	Solid	Firm	Tough
Feel	Hold	Flow	Rub
Grasp	Texture	Move	Itchy
Grab	Quality	Snap	Dig
Get hold of	Pressure	Smooth	Uptight
Unfeeling	Catch	Rough	Handle

Some people will also operate from a mix of two systems called auditory-digital and that's where they listen to what is said and then repeat the question in their minds before answering. Auditory-digital people want factual data, they consider the theoretical implications through logical analysis. They tend to use non sensory words, words that are neutral with regard to any particular sensory system.

Auditory-digital words

Question	Think	Special	Idea
Sense	Know	Basic	Decide
Process	Consider	Virtual	Framework
Motivate	Obvious	Learning	Transition
Learn	Logical	Typical	Compatible
Random	Knowledge	Tendency	Procedure

Let's say you mainly operate from a visual perspective. For a couple of weeks, practise being in the auditory, kinesthetic or auditory-digital systems, then switch to the other system, keep rotating them so that it becomes more natural to operate between each one without thinking too much about it. You will find you get more naturally in rapport with people in your communicating – especially if you match yourself to their preferred system.

Real life story

A good friend and client once said, while we were having a conversation about life in general, that he had read a quote on Facebook,

"You are who you are due to the choices you made in the past: who you are married to or living with, your job, your house or just your life as is. Looking back briefly to the choices you made in the past will give learnings for the future."

He said, "This simple statement gave me insight into the hidden or forgotten issues I had i.e. trust and always wanting to be seen as being right!"

I found it curious that he said this, as we had often talked about this subject before, about how your past is creating your future until you put your past firmly in the past. It wasn't until he read the quote, however, that he could see what was in his blind spot, out of his view.

His preferred representation system is visual, so even though we had spoken about it (auditory), it wasn't until he saw it written down that the message got home for him.

Maybe something you see as you read this book will trigger answers for you?

When you become more aware of these main representation systems, you begin to expand your own knowledge and learning abilities. You also have olfactory and gustatory senses: smell and taste, though most people operate generally within the main four.

It is said that at any moment there are only six things you could be doing inside your head: seeing pictures (visual), hearing sounds (auditory), having feelings (kinesthetic), talking to yourself (auditory-digital), smelling (olfactory), or tasting (gustatory).

YOUR UNANSWERED QUESTIONS

You already know how to learn...

> You learned how to walk, talk, read and write, did you not?
> They are all skills, so where can you go now?
> What can you learn to do now?

Dealing with accusations – Real life story

I had a client who was accused of stealing money in her work environment, resulting in her losing her job. This in turn left her feeling angry, hurt and ashamed of what other people would think, even though she was innocent of the accusation.

Due to these very strong emotions she had sleepless nights, she put on weight due to comfort eating and at one point had become so low she took an overdose.

In our sessions we worked at letting go of all the emotions she had attached to the whole event and the meanings that had been put to it. With EFT we worked through the down feeling she had in the middle part of her body, her fear of going out, and those started to resolve. We used some NLP techniques to take the charge out of some recurring images she was experiencing, and then used hypnosis to work on building self esteem, confidence, acceptance and forgiveness (trees and branches again.) She also listened to my relaxation change CD between sessions, and after we finished working together.

After our sessions she began sleeping better, she lost weight, and says she feels much better.

Bad Habits

Habits such as nail biting start with an initial sensitising event that forms into the habit. Bad habits – or really habits that we no longer want – usually have triggers that set off our unconscious patterns.

Some people tolerate them all their lives or choose to keep them. Others make a decision to change something and get rid of the unwanted habit. Whatever it is, you can let it go.

Some people get a pay-off of some kind from their habit such as feeling better or getting relief in some way. Many habits are unconscious and formed early on in life: you don't even realise you are doing it for a while, and then you may become annoyed at yourself for doing it in the first place. It's a never-ending cycle you just can't seem to break away from – but with the right tools anything is possible.

Habits usually begin as harmless enough, but over time patterns can form around this habit which in turn hold the habit in place. You have to become aware of the patterns you have created, and then do something differently to break these patterns, and let go of the habit – if you so desire.

A smoker may have habits of having a cigarette with a coffee or first thing when they get up in the morning or after a meal, or to be sociable with others who smoke, etc.

A nail biter/chewer could daydream and automatically begin to nibble away on a nail and before they know it have chewed most nails away. They are all patterns of behaviours which create habits. They can be changed with tools from this book.

First, become more aware of the feelings and thoughts prior to indulging in your habit. This will give you insights as to why you have your habit – then you can choose to keep it or let it go.

To loosen habits, ask yourself:

> In what situations does this habit occur?
> What am I feeling when this habit arises?
> What can I do differently that will have me change this pattern?
> How can I change this habit?
> What tools will help me change this habit?
> Can I do it myself?
> Do I need help?

Tools that may help (see section two for descriptions)

EFT, NLP, subliminal therapy, and hypnosis can work well to alleviate unwanted habits, especially using a combination of the above tools.

Pregnancy and childbirth

I highly recommend hypnosis here. We all know that being relaxed through pregnancy and childbirth is beneficial to both mother and baby. Most relaxation is taught on a conscious level. When taught self-hypnosis and unconscious relaxation, the experience of pregnancy and childbirth can be totally different and more enjoyable.

I've seen this over and over again with women and their partners I have worked with, throughout this miraculous process: bringing life into the world – and before you ladies start shouting, "What does he know?" I have been through it five times, albeit not from your perspective ...

I have worked with members of my own family through their own pregnancies with great success. Rather than me try to tell you about it, here is what my daughter, Nichola, says:

I was overjoyed in January 2009 when my husband and I found out that we were to expect our first child. This amazing feeling however quickly became overshadowed by my overwhelming fear of childbirth. Being a little bit of a control freak, not loving the idea of childbirth and being adamant that only a natural birth would do, I knew I needed help!! I began reading and researching all about childbirth, finding out as much as I could about the different options available and drawing on other women's experiences. One subject that came to my attention was using hypnotherapy as a tool to make childbirth as easy as possible. Having a dad who is a qualified practitioner was perfect!

After just three sessions, not only had I overcome my fear, but both my husband and I were trained in techniques that would allow us to create a calm and peaceful environment into which our little one could be born.

The result? A short labour (for a first timer!!) with only gas and air and TENS machine as pain relief! So peaceful and calm was the process that both my own and baby's heart beats stayed consistent throughout. After all the fear and anxiety, I actually enjoyed the whole experience! I even managed some singing, chatting and dancing on the fit ball!!

We now have a beautiful daughter who is very much looking forward to becoming a big sister. I can now enjoy this pregnancy without fear, and with the comfort that we have all the tools we need to experience an equally special moment in time with our second child.

Thank you for giving us such a special gift, Dad,

All our love,

Nic, Jas, Brooke & Baby Bump! XXxx

And this from another daughter, Johanna:

Dad, thank you so much for the strength you helped me to find to get me through giving birth to my daughter. As you know, I was quite apprehensive during my last few weeks of pregnancy but due to the sessions I had with you my labour went very smoothly. In fact the midwives couldn't believe how well I was doing without any pain relief.

When I was 8cm dilated one midwife actually said, "You can't be, you look far too good and relaxed"!

Thanks again,

Johanna.

Tools that may help (see section two for descriptions)

Hypnosis, EFT, visualisation

Health issues

Asthma, eczema, psoriasis, migraines, hay fever, high blood pressure, muscle spasms, nervous ticks, stammers, etc. are all things that have developed as you grew up. After all, how many of these were you born with?

Useful questions to ask yourself, to develop awareness and begin to address these things are:

>Where did it start?
>At what time in my life did it begin?
>What was going on in my world at that time?
>What decision did I make about what was going on?

A client and I had been exploring different events from his life at specific times. After a couple of sessions I asked the question again, "When did this begin?"

"About three years ago."

"What happened three years ago?"

It came out that his grandfather, someone he was very close to, had passed away. He couldn't see until that moment that this had been a major factor in triggering the dis-ease he was experiencing at that present time.

Many clients I work with find that there are incompletions around the loss of someone even twenty years previous, which are having profound effects on their health in some way.

Could this be true for you?

Tools that may help (see section two for descriptions)

Reiki can be very useful for health issues.

Once again, it depends on the underlying issues – have a look through section two to see which tools seem right for you. As a general rule, EFT, NLP and hypnosis are very effective in most situations.

And, as always, if you are experiencing physical symptoms which are bothering you, it is a good idea to visit your GP.

Self-esteem issues

Insecurity, inferiority, self-hate, self-pity, not feeling good about yourself, not loving and accepting yourself etc. Again, something, somewhere, at some point initiated the way you feel about yourself.

Even if you know what started it, you may not realise how the patterns have formed from this event, and how easily many of these patterns can be changed, leaving you more empowered, more confident and feeling much better about yourself, permanently,

Questions to ask yourself:

> Why do I choose to feel low?
>
> How do I feel when I feel better about myself?
>
> What are some things I like about myself?
>
> What is it that I can build on with the things I do like about myself?
>
> What do my friends like about me?
>
> What stops me taking on compliments?

Getting to the root of the issue:

> What was happening in my life when this started?
>
> Was there any significant event that may have triggered things?
>
> Were there any disruptions?

How am I thinking when I don't feel good?

What is my self-talk when I feel that low feeling?

These questions will help you start to become aware of what is at the root of these feelings.

Tools that may help (see section two for descriptions)

Personal development will help you become more confident. As always, EFT, hypnosis and NLP; and other tools as required.

Jealousy

The green-eyed monster is a very destructive emotion, especially in personal relationships. It is very restrictive, can involve being controlling and mistrusting (there is our tree and branches growing again) and unless resolved will push the other person away.

The one holding onto the jealousy will continue to get uncomfortable feelings that are far too strong for logical thinking and can affect their health in the long term.

The feeling of jealousy will usually originate in your early years, generally from relationships with parents, siblings, friends or a first passionate relationship. This is one of your typical trees that will grow many branches (attachments) if not caught and dealt with early on. It can lay dormant within you and then get triggered unexpectedly with all sorts of irrational behaviours showing up.

But it's never too late to resolve it – it is simply a matter of being aware of what is going on inside you and making a choice about what you will do.

I know of many people who dislike their partners going out and socialising in other company without them, or phone them regularly to check on their whereabouts (how energy sapping is that for all involved?)

The thing is, because this feeling may have been developed early on in life, the person will not make the connection to earlier decisions and experiences, and will live life as if this feeling is the norm, along with the behaviours that are hurtful and damaging to their relationships.

I AM HERE TO LET YOU KNOW THEY ARE NOT THE NORM AND CAN BE CHANGED WITH SOME EFFORT FROM YOU!

Is jealousy an issue for you? Answer these questions:

> How many times have you accused your partner of something you made up that turned out to be an untruth?
> Have you laid awake at night while your partner was out socialising, and thinking all the wrong things?
> How many rows and arguments have developed because of your thoughts and feelings around jealousy?
> Are you a compulsive phone checker, looking to see who has been texting them?

It's time to get a grip and let go of that destructive feeling.
> What would it be like to be free of that old, gut-wrenching, soul-destroying, harmful jealous feeling?

Once you are free of that old jealous feeling, relationships and life will work much better for you and you will be far more empowered within your own life. No more jealous feeling.

> What will it be like to be free of this destructive state?

An exercise to tackle jealousy

This is a variation on the releasing uncomfortable or negative feelings exercise in section two.

> Find a quiet place where you will not be interrupted.
> Bring that jealous feeling up.
> Thank your unconscious mind for bringing it to your attention.
> Make that jealous feeling as intense as you can – again, this is part of the process, and will pass.
> Rate the feeling 0 to 10, 10 being the worst it can be.
> Then ask yourself:
>> When was the first time I experienced this feeling?
>> What happened for me to experience this feeling?
>> Who was I with?
>> What did they do?
>
> Then go through the following:
>> If the jealousy had a colour, what would it be?
>> If it had a shape what shape is it?
>> What about the texture?
>> What about the temperature?
>> Does it move or is it still?
>> Does it have any sound?
>
> Once you have full awareness of this, change the colour to something more comforting, change the shape, get a sense of

what happens to the temperature, if it was moving make it still, if it's still make it move, use your wonderful imagination to visualise these changes, or if visualising is difficult for you then get a sense of the changes.

Think about the jealousy, now see how it's changed, you are now changing the state you are in and you can do this with any state any time.

Now rate the feeling again from 0 to 10, and notice how it is coming down.

Tools that may help (see section two for descriptions)

EFT is a great technique to use to resolve jealousy. If you haven't learned it already, I suggest going to a qualified practitioner to learn the technique, and then using it yourself as needed.

Using EFT, tap on all the different aspects that come up when asking questions of yourself; trust your unconscious mind to help you. Be patient, you may get memories in images or just get a sense of something you had forgotten about – it may be something you know about but just had not recognised the patterns that had formed, or what started it all off.

At some point you will have a break-through and begin to let go of those jealous feelings – or maybe completely let go for good! Again, EFT, NLP and hypnotherapy, and many of the other tools in section two can help set you free from those chains.

Loneliness

Being alone can be difficult for some people, usually a feeling in the chest, an empty feeling. If you remember my story of kick-a-tin, you'll remember how I made the decision that I was all alone and unloved.

Once you are aware of the pattern you have created of lonely feelings, you can let go and fill this space with something more satisfying, fulfilling like love, comfort or whatever works for you.

Many people tend to move away from such a feeling by finding company, distraction, whatever they have found that eases the feeling.

Instead, it can help to face the feeling. Refer to section two, releasing uncomfortable or negative feelings, for a process to help you let go of the negative feelings of loneliness

Sports performance - better golf, rugby, football, darts, snooker, tennis, boxing etc.

Many professionals use hypnosis to better their performances within their specific discipline, especially with regard to visualisation.

You could be held back in some way by situations or decisions from your past conditioning. It is not always necessary to trawl back through all the situations that have joined to create your limiting blocks (whether you are aware of them or not). You can, however, use the various tools in this book – yourself, to some extent or with an appropriate professional – and make amazing advances in any sport.

Questions to ask to improve performance:

> What stops me being the best that I can be?
> What self-limitations am I putting on myself?
> Am I afraid to win?
> What would happen if I won?
> Do I want to be the best?
> Am I dedicated enough?
> How much do I really want this?
> What is the one thing that is holding me back?

Life is like a huge puzzle and when the right parts are brought together a clear picture is formed.

I have helped many people in many disciplines to move blocks that have been holding them back.

Real life story

One young man, Tyler, was eight years old when his parents brought him to see me. He had recently been accepted into a local Academy of Excellence for football.

Tyler, a talented young man, was experiencing some problems with aspects of his game.

As we worked together it became apparent that Tyler had experienced a nasty tackle, and was also having some verbal bullying at school.

Using hypnosis, EFT, visualisation and story telling, Tyler was able to set himself free from his limiting decisions and feelings, enabling him to excel at what he wants to achieve and what he does best in his game.

Children are great to work with as they have fewer trees in their fields to knock down and usually get this work really quickly. The earlier and more quickly you deal with these patterns, the less attachments are made throughout life, helping you to stay healthier and happier.

Tyler, now eleven, has been invited to stay at the academy for the next stages and has accepted the invitation. He has been told his skills are exceptional.

Time will tell. Will he be a new Welsh footy wizard?

Golfers sometimes get what is called the shanks or the yips where they have trouble with their shots or their putting.

Darters have trouble letting go of their darts (dartisis).

Footballers go off their game, or in rugby a player may begin to miss penalties or conversions. Some of this is down to focus – remember, an emotion can be many more times stronger than logic, so it may not make any sense to that sports person, but something somewhere within them is going on. In my experience, something in mind or body or both is usually out of balance, and that is affecting that person's performance and results.

Tools that may help (see section two for descriptions)

Visualisation. Try this:

> Relax and visualise yourself doing the things you want to do, and being the way you want to be. Go into your future and see things being achieved exactly as you want them to be achieved.

Visualisation is well documented amongst the sporting fraternity, and some sports people have changed their visualisation from, instead of seeing themselves achieving at some element of their sport (disassociated) to seeing as if through their own eyes actually achieving what they want (associated). This alone has made the difference for some in winning instead of coming second or third. This method can also be used for many other aspects of life.

Relaxation through trance. I have worked with sports people who, as we go through the processes I use, have realised a tension in their legs or arms that they were not aware of. Through the process of using the tools and techniques in this book we eliminate these tensions, they relax more into their sport and their game improves, giving them more focus and improving their skills.

Paul's Progress

Before we finish, a last note: I promised when I told his story at the beginning of the book that I would tell you about Paul's progress.

Paul has made tremendous progress and is becoming more independent. He is able to feed himself, dress himself and walk out of the hydrospa unassisted. He has even had a driving lesson on private land – not on the road yet!

He is in a position that the experts thought he would never get to, and his progress continues. He is an inspiration!

~~~~~~~~~~~~~~~~~~~~~~~~~~~~~~

Ymdrechir ac fe lwyddir – endeavour and you will succeed.

~~~~~~~~~~~~~~~~~~~~~~~~~~~~~~

Thank you for reading

Your Unanswered Questions

If you have had any issues come up, or if anything is concerning you after reading this book, or if you have simply enjoyed it and would like to tell me, then please email me at
stephentruelove1@yahoo.co.uk
I will be happy to put you on the path to getting what you need. I will also add you to my mailing list so you can receive information about further publications.

Email also if you would like to buy a
copy of my relaxation change CD

Or you can find out more about me at
www.mind-set-solutions.co.uk

Please post your review on
your favourite book or
ebook website

With my very great thanks,

Steve.

Testimonials for Stephen

"I am extremely grateful for the opportunity for a session with Stephen this summer. I had been feeling overwhelmingly unhappy and wasn't aware that there hadn't been any specific events to lead me to feel this way.

"During the session with Stephen, we uncovered certain moments and mindsets that informed the way I thought and behaved. It sounds crazy but after the session my life has completely turned around - my attitude has changed to see things holistically, I feel motivated and grateful every day and have even noticed differences with things like running.

"The single session plus Stephen's suggestions, things like a daily practice in being present and taking time to understand things /thoughts that happen, have really altered my outlook and experiences! Thank you for your help - so hugely appreciated."

Elle McIntyre

"I would personally like to thank Steve Truelove, for all his positive time and support, helping me to successfully see a different way of living.

"As a result of therapy with Steve my anxiety has loosened and I have been led to letting go of unnecessary worries I had every day.

"After each session I always felt better like a little skip was back in my step. His method of therapy is relaxed and down to earth – you can tell him anything and do not worry about what he will think, only that you know he will help in the best way possible.

"I would highly recommend his services to anyone suffering from upsetting/struggling situations. What I have gained has been invaluable and I will be thankful for this every day."

Lauren - Anxiety & OCD Sufferer

Printed in Great Britain
by Amazon.co.uk, Ltd.,
Marston Gate.